QlikView Questions and Answers

Guide to QlikView and FAQs

Chandraish Sinha

Copyright © 2016

www.LearnAllBi.com

Legal Notes

About The Author

Chandraish Sinha has years of experience implementing Business Intelligence solutions. His experience involves working in different business intelligence applications. He worked in many QlikView end-to-end implementations.

He currently holds certification in QlikView designer and QlikView developer.

He coaches organizations and consultants in exploring the awesome world of QlikView.

He has a passion for QlikView and shares his knowledge through his blog (http://LearnAllBi.com).

Chandraish is also the author of QlikView Essentials, a step by step guide on creating QlikView data model and dashboard.

Table of Contents
Preface

Preface

QlikView provides an innovative way to analyze data. The popularity of QlikView is due to the fact that QlikView can extract huge amounts of data and present it in a format that is easy to understand and interpret.

A good understanding on any application requires learning the key concepts.

This book offers a quick understanding of key concepts in Business Intelligence and QlikView. This book explains each concept in a very easy to understand manner. It is presented in a question and answer format. It provides direction and guidance for advanced exploration.

About this book

Chapter1. Understanding the Basics

> These questions are designed to improve the general understanding of the reader. It will cover general concepts in QlikView and Datawarehousing. It also covers the basics of SQL as related to QlikView.

Chapter2. Questions on QlikView developer

> This chapter contains questions on QlikView scripting and data model. It will give a peek into different data modeling concepts in QlikView.

Chapter3. Questions on QlikView designer

> Questions in this chapter will test your knowledge on the visualization aspect of QlikView.

Chapter4. Questions on Server/Admin

> This chapter contains questions on dashboard deployment and other server related tasks.

Chapter5. Commonly Asked Questions

> This chapter contains commonly asked questions in QlikView.

How to use this Book

This book is designed in a Question and answer format. The best way to use this book is to go through all the questions and try to understand the concepts and exercises.

To recreate scenario's presented in this book, download QlikView desktop personal edition. QlikView desktop can be downloaded for free from

http://www.qlik.com/try-or-buy/download-qlikview

Choose the 32-bit or 64-bit version based on your windows version. QlikView desktop personal edition comes with the complete functionality of QlikView.

To practice the concepts, create the tables mentioned in the section **"Data used in the book"**

Readers can also download any sample databases available online or SQL server sample databases. Data in any excel or csv file can also be used to explore QlikView functionality.

To practice exercises, feel free to create multiple QlikView Qvw files with charts and scripts as needed.

Who needs to read this book and why?

Want to brush up QlikView concepts?

Looking for scenario based questions?

New to QlikView and want to grasp all the key concepts?

QlikView expert and want to test your knowledge?

If you answered YES to the above questions, then this book is for you.

This book will help QlikView learners in understanding the basics of QlikView. The book is designed for developers to get a quick understanding of QlikView. This book will prepare readers for any technical discussion on QlikView. Seasoned developers can also test their knowledge. This book should work as a guide and encouragement for further exploration.

Data used in the book

To recreate exercises in this book,

Create the following tables in excel or database and load them in QlikView.

To explain various concepts, these tables may be loaded in different exercises in different forms. You may create multiple QVWs to recreate the scenarios.

To load tables in QlikView, follow first, second and third questions in Chap2. Questions on QlikView Developer

TestTable

ID	Year	Name	Address	Product	Amount
ID1	2012	John	Mount Street	Shirt	100
ID2	2013	Smith	Link Street	Pant	200
ID3	2014	Leena	Cobb Street	Socks	300

Prescriber

Prescriber ID	SalesRepID	NoofCalls	ProductsSold	Amount
P1	S1	5	10	100
P2	S2	10	25	200
P3	S3	15	15	150

VendorCall

SalesRepID	VendorName	NoofCalls	ProductsSold	Amount
S1	CVS	30	10	50
S2	WallsGreen	40	15	25
S3	MediCentre	50	30	40

SalesRep

SalesRepID	Name
S1	Mike
S2	Tom
S3	Sheldon

Chapter 1.
Understanding the
Basics

Q. What is QlikView?
Ans.

- QlikView is an in-memory Business Intelligence application. In-memory means data is loaded and queried from RAM.
- QlikView uses the associative technology. Tables having common fields are associated or linked.
- QlikView stores data at a granular level. Data is not pre-aggregated.
- Components of QlikView are QlikView desktop and Server/Publisher and Access point.
- The developer uses QlikView desktop to write scripts. Scripts are used to extract data from the data source and design data model. QlikView desktop is also used to create dashboard/visualizations.
- Dashboards are deployed on the Server. Publisher, a component of server, helps in data load, data reduction and scheduling.
- Business users view Dashboards through Access point portal.
- The file extension of the QlikView design file is .qvw.

Q. What is Business Intelligence? How QlikView is a BI application.
Ans.

- BI or Business Intelligence is a general term used to categorize software applications that help in analyzing and understanding data. Such applications enable business users in making useful decisions.
- These applications include functionalities such as ETL (Extract, transform and load) data and creating visualizations in terms of charts and tables.
- QlikView is a BI application because QlikView has a strong scripting engine that performs ETL. It can take the raw data, transform it and provide highly interactive visualization objects to help in executive decision making.

Q. Why QlikView is required in today's business world?

Ans.

Every business has tons of data. This data can be in different formats like database, excel, xml and so on.

- QlikView can connect to any data format.
- It can connect to different data formats such as excel and database table in one dashboarding application.
- QlikView can handle huge amounts of data.
- QlikView helps in extracting/transforming and interpreting this data.
- Using associative technology, QlikView automatically identifies the relationship between the data and presents in a format – charts/tables that is understandable to the users.
- It helps business in discovering data and making decisions.

Q. How association works in QlikView

Ans.

- In QlikView, an association is formed between 2 tables based on common field names.
- There can be only one link between the tables, i.e. there can be only one common field between the tables.
- Synthetic key is formed, if more than one common field is present between the tables.
- The association helps in leading to the data directly, unlike other tools which follow a predefined path.

Q. What is Green, White and Gray concept in QlikView?

Ans.

On a QlikView dashboard, when user selects a data item on the screen, selected data element is highlighted in Green, associated data element is displayed as white and non-associated data element is shown in gray.

Selected Data	Associated Data	Not associated data

Q. What data sources can be used with QlikView?
Ans.
QlikView can connect to a variety of data sources. It can connect to Excel sheets, Text files, xml, web files, relational database or a data warehouse. QlikView can connect to these data sources in one design/Qvw file. It automatically identifies the relationship between the data based on the common field names.

Q. What is Access Point?
Ans.
The access point is a portal through which users can access dashboards. Access point works with clients like AJAX or IE Plug-in. No installation is required for AJAX client. The IE plugin requires installation.

Q. What is QlikView Development life cycle?
Ans.
The typical QlikView implementation follows:
- Requirement gathering. Discussion with users to understand data and visualization requirements.
- Analyze data sources. Gather information on different data sources and the relationships among the data elements.
- Create mock-ups of the dashboards. User review of mock-ups
- Create data model.
- Create dashboards
- Unit Testing.
- Review of dashboard by the users.
- Deploy dashboards over the Server.
- Create data load and dashboard distribution tasks.
- Publish dashboards to be viewed over access point.

Q. What are dimensions and facts? What is the cardinality between them?
Ans.
Dimension and fact tables are used in describing a star schema.

- Dimension table contains the text attribute **of** the data. It provides the context to Fact table. Dimensions are used to filter the fact table.
- Fact table contains the measurable attribute of the data. Such as Revenue, Profit or Population.
- In a star schema, fact is in the center surrounded by different dimensions.
- The cardinality between Dimension and a fact table is one to Many, with Many on the fact side.

Q. Given an ER diagram, how you will identify fact and dimension tables
Ans.

- Cardinality between Dimension and Fact is one to many, with many on the Fact side. Look for One to Many relationship in the ER diagram.
- Dimension contain the textual/ descriptive attribute and Fact contain the measured data. Look for such data elements in the tables.
- Fact table contains the foreign key of the dimension table.

Q. How requirement gathering is performed for a Dashboarding application?
Ans.
When creating a dashboard, it is important to get the requirements from the users. When gathering requirements,

- Take data requirements. Data sources, key filters, data refresh frequency.
- Inquire users about the KPI's (Key performance Indicators).
- Understand what questions users are trying to get from the data.
- Document business rules required for the dashboards.
- Understand security requirements.
- Gather details about any existing reports or desired visualization.

- Provide the look or screen layout of the dashboard charts and tables in excel or hand drawn. Get users' feedback on the layout.
- Get requirements about the screen resolution.

Q. What is a KPI?
Ans.
Key Performance Indicator or KPI is a key measure/s that is used by an organization to evaluate performance. KPI's are different for different organizations, for example, for a retail company, one for the KPI may be Sales Amount, for a hospital, it may be number of patients treated.

Q. How source control is performed in QlikView
Ans.
Starting with version 11, QlikView can be integrated to source control applications like Microsoft TFS (Team Foundation Server) and subversion.

Q. How two tables are linked in QlikView?
Ans.
In QlikView, two tables are linked based on common field names between the two tables.

Q. What's the difference between a primary key and foreign key in SQL?
Ans.
Primary key uniquely identifies a record in a table. Primary key in one table is referenced by a foreign key in another table. Two relational tables are linked based on primary key and foreign key.

Q. What are some of the joins in SQL?
Ans.
The joins in SQL are

- Inner Join. Returns matching rows from both the tables.
- Left/Outer join. Returns all rows from the left table and the matched rows from the right table.
- Right/Outer join. Returns all rows from the Right table and the matched rows from the left table.
- Full/Outer join. Returns all rows from table1 and from the table2. It combines the result of both LEFT and RIGHT joins.
- Cartesian join. Join of every row of one table to every row of another table.

Q. What is the Group By clause in SQL?
Ans.
Group By is always used with Aggregation functions. It groups the query result by one or more columns. Columns in SQL statement containing Group By should be used with aggregation functions or should be under Group By clause.

Q. What is Composite key?
Ans.
It is a combination of 2 or more fields in a table that can be used to uniquely identify each row in the table.

Q. What is the difference between Union and Union All in SQL?
Ans.
Union and Union All are used to combine results of queries. Union eliminates the duplicate records and Union All includes all the records.

Q. What is meant by data transformation?

Ans.

Data transformation means transforming the data from its original format. Raw data may be in a different format then required by the report or dashboard. Data transformation is required to make the data more suited for the application. An example, will be to remove time information from the DateTime.

Q. What is data granularity?

Ans.

Data granularity refers to the level of detail or depth of data. It means the level at which data is stored in the fact table. For e.g. if data is stored at the Year level, then it is at the lower granularity. If the data is stored at the Month or day level, then it at higher granularity.

Q. What is the difference between Star schema and Snow flake scheme?

Ans. In Star schema, Fact table is in the center and surrounded by dimension tables. Snow flake schema is similar to star schema. In Snow flake schema, dimension tables may be connected to other related dimensions. For example, City dimension may connect to address dimension.

Q. How data is stored internally in QlikView

Ans.

QlikView internally stores data in two levels. First level stores distinct lists of value and the second level contains pointers to these values.

Data is stored in a field only once. For example, if the City is present in multiple tables in your database, it will be stored only once in QlikView. This is very useful in large datasets, where repeated values are stored only once.

Chapter 2.
Questions on QlikView developer

Q. How data is extracted in QlikView

Ans.

In QlikView, data is extracted by writing scripts. Various load statements are used in scripts to extract data.

Scripts are written in Script editor. To write scripts, launch QlikView desktop and press Ctrl + E to invoke the script editor. Data can be extracted from the database by using an OLEDB/ODBC connection or from files such as excel, text files or QVDs.

Q. What steps should be followed to load the database tables in QlikView?

Ans.

To load data from a database table,

- Launch QlikView desktop. Use Ctrl + E to initiate script editor.
- Create an ODBC or OLEDB connection to the database.
- In the script editor, from the bottom tabs, select **Data** tab and click on **connect.**
- Create database connection and select tables.
- Once the table is selected Load script is automatically generated.
- As a best practice, always name your table. The Table is referenced by Table name throughout the script. The syntax is TableName: or [Table Name]: depending on if the table name contains a space or no space.
- Click on the **Reload** icon from the menu or Ctrl + R to load data.

Q. What steps should be followed to load table files such as excel, text file or QVDs

Ans.

To load the table files,

- Launch QlikView desktop. Use Ctrl + E to initiate script editor.
- In the script editor, from the tab at the bottom select **Table files** and browse to your files.

- Once the file is selected, load statement is automatically generated.
- As a best practice, always name your table. The Table is referenced by Table name throughout the script. The syntax is TableName: or [Table Name]: depending on if the table name contains a space or no space.
- Click on the **Reload** icon from the menu or Ctrl + R to load data.

If TestTable.xlsx, mentioned in the beginning of this book is loaded, the load script will look like

```
TestTable: //Name of the table
LOAD
        ID,
        Year,
        Name,
        Address,
        Product,
        Amount
FROM
TestTable.xlsx
(ooxml, embedded labels, table is TestTable);
```

TestTable in the last line, is the name of the sheet tab in excel

Q. How loaded tables and data model can be viewed?
Ans.
Once the data is loaded, use **Table viewer** to see the loaded table.
- Table viewer can be invoked by clicking on the Table Viewer icon from the menu or by using Ctrl + T.
- Table viewer displays the loaded table with fields. If multiple tables are loaded, it shows how tables are linked.
- You can get a preview of the table data. Hover over the table, to display other important attributes of the table.

Q. What approach should be followed in creating a data model?
Ans.
- The data model is created by extracting data and applying transformations.
- The data model should be designed by using QVDs (QlikView Data Files). A table of data should be extracted and stored in a QVD. While creating visualization, data should be read from the QVD as reading/writing data from QVD provides better performance.
- A multi-tier architecture should be followed while creating data model. This involves creating a **data layer** to extract raw data from tables and storing it in QVD.
- In **Transform layer**, data transformation is applied.
- In **Presentation layer**, data from the QVDs are read to create visualizations.
- While loading data from multiple tables, synthetic keys and loops may be formed. Synthetic keys and loops should be resolved.
- Data model should be clean with less number of tables.

Q. What problems can occur when multiple tables are extracted in QlikView?
Ans.
When multiple tables are loaded in QlikView, sometimes Synthetic keys or loops are formed.

Q. What is synthetic key and how it is resolved?
Ans.
Synthetic key is formed by the presence of more than one common field between the two more tables.
There are different ways to resolve a synthetic key. Depending on the specific scenario, any of the following techniques can be used
- Ensure that only required fields connect.
- Alias the column that is not required to be linked.
- Comment column/s in a table that are not required in the dashboard.
- Use Qualify and UnQualify statements.

- Concatenate tables.
- Create Link table.
- Concatenate key fields to create a composite key.

Q. Load Prescriber, VendorCall and SalesRep tables. Table structures are provided in the beginning of the book. See the following tables in the Table Viewer. Identify problem in the data model and suggest a solution.

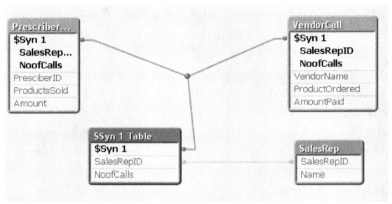

Ans.
- The data model diagram, shows synthetic/Syn_1 table creation. This table is formed due to the presence of more than one common field between Prescriber and VendorCall tables. These fields are SalesRepID and NoofCalls.
- Synthetic key should be avoided in this case. To resolve the synthetic key, rename one of the columns.
- SalesRepID should not be renamed as it is used for linking the tables.
- NoofCalls column can be renamed. It is clear from the data model that NoofCalls in Prescriber table is different than the NoofCalls of calls in the Vendor table. NoofCalls in the prescriber table means calls made to the prescriber and NoofCalls in the Vendor table mean Calls made to the Vendor. So renaming NoofCalls will have no impact on the overall data model.

Q. What will happen when the following tables are loaded in QlikView?

Auto	Customer	Shipper
AutoID	AutoID	CustomerID
Name	CustomerID	Name
AutoName	Date	ShipDate
UnitPrice	SaleAmount	Freight

Ans.

If above tables are loaded, the loop will get created. Script execution window will show a warning about the loop creation. The loop gets created when more than one path exist between the tables. Loop creates ambiguity. The loop should be avoided. In this model, **Name** in Auto table has a different context than **Name** in the Shipper table. Name in the Auto table refer to the Auto seller company name. Name in Shipper table refers to the Shipper Company. We can rename one of the columns and then load the data. This will resolve the circular loop.

Q. What is a QVD?
Ans.

- QVD stands for QlikView Data File. It contains the data extracted from the data source table.
- QVD is a native QlikView format. Read/write to QVD can only be done from QlikView.
- Reading data from a QVD file is faster than reading from a database table.
- QVD can store any kind of data viz. Database, excel or text file. QVD file has .qvd extension. It is created using the **Store** command.
- Data is read from QVD using the load command

Q. Why and how QVDs are used
Ans.

- It is faster to read data from a QVD file.
- In QlikView script, data can be extracted from the table and stored in a QVD file.

- Use multiple QVD files to create the efficient data model. Create dashboards by reading data from the QVD instead of data source.
- QVD creation and data storage is done by using the **STORE** command. Unless a path is specified, generated QVD resides in the same folder as the qvw file.
- Reading data from QVD is similar to reading from Table files such as xls or csv

Q. How you will create and store TestTable into a QVD

Ans. Load the table and use Store command to create QVD. QVD will get created in the same location as qvw file.

TestTable:
LOAD
    ID,
    Year,
    Name,
    Address,
    Product,
    Amount
FROM
TestTable.xlsx
(ooxml, embedded labels, table is TestTable);

STORE TestTable into TestTable.Qvd;

Q. Name some of the functions used in creating a data model?

Ans.

Functions or statements are used to get the required functionality. QlikView provides a wide range of functions. Some of the functions used in scripts are

- **Load** is used to load the data from the data source.
- **Store** is used to create and load data into QVD.
- **Mapping** Load is used to create Mapping Table.
- **ApplyMap** is used with Mapping load to map the expression or column to the table.

- **Peek** is used to return the value of a field in a specific row in a table.
- **Autonumber** is used to get distinct integer value of an expression. It can be used to convert concatenation of fields resulting in a string to an integer.
- **Concatenate** appends the two tables. The resulting table will have a sum of the number of rows of table one plus the sum of the rows of the table two.
- **Year** and **Month** are used to get Year and Month from a date.

Q. How two tables are joined in QlikView?
Ans.
Two tables are joined by the use of the **Join** statement in the script. The join between the two tables is a single table containing the output of the join. Join can be inner, left, right or outer join.

Q. How Keep differs from a Join
Ans.
In QlikView, the result of a Join between 2 tables is one table containing the output of the join. Join between two tables is made based on the matching column.
Join and **Keep** have the same functionality except that join results in one table, whereas Keep contains two tables. It creates an output table, but also keeps the table which prefix keep by **left** or **right**.

Q. What is concatenate? What is a similar database/SQL key word?
Ans.
Concatenate or concatenation of tables in QlikView is similar to Union All in SQL.
Concatenate appends the 2 tables and creates one table. The resulting column has the sum of columns of table 1 plus the sum of columns of table 2.
Concatenate has 3 flavors
- Automatic concatenation. When the number of columns and name of columns in the 2 tables are same, they are automatically concatenated.

- Forced Concatenation. If number and the name of the columns are not same, force concatenation can be performed by using **concatenate** keyword between two tables.
- NoConcatenate. To avoid the automatic concatenation use **NoConcatenate** key word between the tables.

Q. What is the difference between Join and concatenate?
Ans.
- Result of a join between two tables in one table.
- In QlikView, Join can be defined as inner, outer, left and right. Join merges tables based on the join criteria or matching rows.
- Unlike Join, Concatenate appends one table into another table.
- Join adds columns and Concatenate add rows

Q. Table1 and Table2 have 2 columns Dim and Sales. What will be the result, when the following tables are loaded into a QlikView Document?

Table1

Dim	Sales
A	100
B	200
C	300

Table2

Dim	Sales
D	400
C	500
E	600

Ans.
After loading Table1 and Table2, output will be only one Table i.e. Table1 in QlikView. Since number and the name of the columns are same, they will get automatically concatenated. The number of rows in resulting Table1 will be 6. It will be the sum of the rows of Table1 + Table2

Q. What is Resident load?
Ans.
Resident load is used to load fields from the already loaded table.
Resident load is required, in case, some additional transformation
or aggregation needs to be performed on the already loaded
table/fields.

Q. See below, TestTable is loaded in QlikView. Due to some
requirement, you want to use the Name field and create a separate
table. How you will achieve this task.
Ans.
TestTable load statement:

```
TestTable:
LOAD
        ID,
        Year,
        Name,
        Address,
        Product,
        Amount
FROM
TestTable.xlsx
(ooxml, embedded labels, table is TestTable);
```

To load Name column from this table, you need not load TestTable
again from the data source. You can instead use **Resident** load to
load Name from the existing TestTable

```
TestTable2:
Load
        Name As NewName
Resident TestTable;
```

Q. What is preceding load in QlikView?
Ans.

- Preceding load allows you to perform multiple transformations in one load script.
- Preceding load takes the input from the previous load statement.
- Multiple load statements can be stacked one top of another, each performing a transformation by taking input from the previous load.
- It also allows the use QlikView functions

Q. Consider the load statement of TestTable. Your requirement is to transform the Amount field and store it in the TestTable as NewAmount.
Ans.

This requirement can be achieved by using preceding load. See below, observe two load statements. The upper load statement is taking the input from the prior load statement. The resulting table will have an additional column for NewAmount

TestTable:
Load *,
Amount *2 As NewAmount;
LOAD
ID,
Year,
Name,
Address,
Product,
Amount
FROM
TestTable.xlsx
(ooxml, embedded labels, table is TestTable);

Q. How to rename all the columns of a table with one statement?
Ans.
Qualify Statement is used to rename all the columns of a table. It can also be used to resolve synthetic keys. Qualify in the load script, qualifies each field in the table, such as, tablename.fieldname. QlikView will continue to qualify till **Unqualify** statement is encountered. You can Unqualify specific field/s such as key fields which are used for association with other tables.

Q. Refer TestTable, how you will use Qualify and UnQualify statements in the load of this table
Ans.

> **QUALIFY *;**
> **UNQUALIFY** ID;
> TestTable:
> LOAD
> > ID,
> > Year,
> > Name,
> > Address,
> > Product,
> > Amount
> FROM
> TestTable.xlsx
> (ooxml, embedded labels, table is TestTable);
>
> **UNQUALIFY;**

Q. How to create a calculated field in QlikView?
Ans.
Creating calculated fields in QlikView is done by using any existing field in the load script and applying the calculation.
In the below example, calculated field NewName is a concatenation of the ID and Name columns.

> TestTable:
> LOAD

ID,
Year,
Name,
ID | | Name As NewName,
Address,
Product,
Amount
FROM
TestTable.xlsx
(ooxml, embedded labels, table is TestTable);

Q. What is a Mapping table in QlikView?
Ans.
It is always a good practice to keep the data model clean with less number of tables and links. If datamodel contains many lookup tables, you can remove them by using Mapping load. Mapping load creates Mapping table.

- **Mapping** table in QlikView is implemented by prefixing load statement with Mapping.
- Mapping table should contain only two columns. One is ID and other column used for mapping the value.
- Use **Apply Map** function to switch the ID with the value.
- Mapping table exists in a separate area in memory and are automatically deleted after script execution.

Q. What technique should be applied to remove Location table in the following data model?

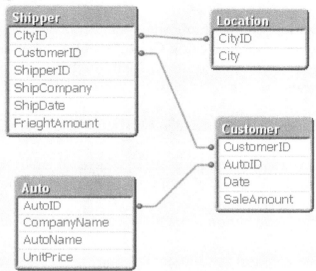

Ans.

Location table is a lookup table and provides City information of Shipper based on CityID.

Location table can be removed by the use of **Mapping** table.

Move the load script of Location table before the Shipper table load script.

Prefix Location load statement with **Mapping** keyword. Your script will look like

```
        City_Map:
        Mapping LOAD
            CityID,
            City
        FROM
        Location.xlsx
        (ooxml, embedded labels, table is ShipperLocation);
```

Navigate to the load script of Shipper table. As a last column use the following ApplyMap statement

```
        ApplyMap('City_Map',CityID,'Missing') As City
```

Don't forget to reload/execute your script by using Crtl + R

Q. How you will incorporate more than one fact table in QlikView?
Ans.
If the data model contains more than one fact table, then these tables can be incorporated using **Concatenate** or **Link** tables.
Use Concatenate when the granularity of the tables are same. Use Link table when the granularity of the tables is different

Q. What is the difference between Link table and Synthetic keys?
Ans.
Link tables are used to resolve synthetic keys which arise due to the presence of multiple fact tables linking to common dimensions.

Q. How to dates are handled in QlikView
Ans.
- Dates are stored as dual data storage i.e. represented by a string and a number. The string is used for display and number is used for calculations.
- QlikView provide number of date and time related functions.
- Date#() is used when Date from the source is represented as string in QlikView. Date# will convert string date into a number.
- Date() is used to convert numeric date into date format.

Q. Why and how Master Calendar is created?
Ans.
In the absence of a Time Dimension, Master Calendar is created in QlikView. It contains all the date related fields in the data model. Master Calendar is created to get continuous dates. Fact table will have dates only when a transaction has occurred, so all dates may not be present in the fact table. In a such a scenario Master Calendar will be useful.
Steps to create a Master Calendar

- Get the Min and Max dates from the fact table or any table that has dates. If more than one table have dates, then pick dates from any one table. This is just to set the start and end points of the dates. **The peek function** can be used to get Min and Max dates.
- Create a Temp table and load the dates between these Min and Max dates. Dates can be generated by using **Autogenerate()** function.
- Create Master Calendar by performing **Resident** load on this Temp Table. Create all the required date fields like Year, Month, Week and so on.
- Join Master Calendar table to the fact table.

Q. How rows can be automatically generated in QlikView
Ans.
Autogenerate function is used to generate rows automatically in QlikView.
The syntax is *Autogenerate number*
The number represents the number of rows to be generated.
Number cannot be an expression that is based on database fields.

Q. How to get the value of the field in a specific row in a QlikView table
Ans.
The **peek** function can be used to get the contents of a field in a specific row.
The syntax is Peek (fieldname, row number,'Table Name')
Row number starts 0 with last row being -1

Q. Consider TestTable loaded in previous exercises. It has 3 names John, Smith and Leena. For some transformation, you want to extract the name on the second row, i.e. Smith and store it in a separate table. How this task can be achieved?
Ans.
Considering TestTable is already loaded. This task can be achieved by using Peek and Resident load

    Second_Name:

Load
        Peek (Name, 1,'TestTable') As Second_Name
    Resident TestTable;

Q. How you will load new and updated rows of data in QlikView data model?
Ans.
In QlikView, new and updated data can be loaded by using **Incremental load** script. Incremental load involves identifying the new records in the data source table and loading only new and update records in QlikView. Incremental load requires the use of QVD.
It has 3 options,

- Insert Only

Insert only option entails, identifying the new records in the table. This is usually done by using RecordUpdateDate or any other flag in the table that identifies a new row. Use such flag to load only those rows which are new and append these rows to the existing QVD by using concatenate

- Insert and Update

Insert and update option is similar to the previous option. With this option load the rows that do not exist in the QVD previously loaded. To achieve this we will follow all the previous steps and to check whether the records already exists in the QVD, we will use NOT EXIST (Key_Field)

- Insert, update and delete

This option is similar to the previous one. In this one we will delete the records from the QVD that are no longer in the data source table. To achieve this we will follow the steps in the second option and perform inner join with the source table.

Q. In which scenario **exists** function is used?
Ans.
Exists can be used any time you want to check if the value getting loaded already exists in QlikView. It is useful while performing incremental load.

Q. Can we call one QlikView dashboard from another?
Ans.
A QlikView dashboard can only inherit the data or scripting part from another dashboard.
Scripts from one dashboard can be reused into other dashboard by using **Binary Load**.
Few restrictions apply on Binary Load:
- Binary load can be performed only on one file i.e. scripts from only one Qvw can be included.
- The binary load statement should be the first statement of the script.
- Using Binary load, one can only load the scripting part, visualizations are never loaded.

If you want to include visualizations from another file, you have to manually copy/paste the visualization from the source to the target dashboard

Q. Multiple developers are creating dashboards out of single data model. How you will ensure that all developers get the same data model and they are not allowed to modify the scripts of the data model
Ans.
Dashboard designers should include data model scripts by using the **Binary load**. In this way all the developers will be using the same data model and script code will not be available for accidental or intentional change.

Q. What is an optimized load of QVD?
Ans.
- Optimized load of QVD is much faster.
- Optimized load occurs if there is no transformation in the script.
- In an optimized load, only Renaming of fields and use of Exists function is allowed.
- Optimized load can be seen in the load script progress window.

- In the presentation layer, optimized load should be done. All transformation should be done in previous layers.

Q. What is Slowly Changing Dimension and how it is implemented in QlikView?
Ans.
Slowly changing dimension or SCD is a data warehousing concept. It deals with keeping the history of the data. An example, of SCD, is an employee changing positions during his employment. You would like to keep a history of all the changes. At database level, this is done by creating multiple records and using start date and end date for each of his positions. Only current position will be open and other previous positions will be ended.
In QlikView, SCD's are implemented by using the interval match function

Q. How to use IN clause in QlikView?
Ans.
In QlikView, the functionality of SQL IN is implemented by using the **Match** function. **WildMatch** function is also available for text comparisons using wild characters. WildMatch performs case-insensitive matches.

Q. Load only those records from the TestTable where Address contains 'O'
Ans.
Load statement for the above requirement will be
        TestTable:
        LOAD
            ID,
            Year,
            Name,
            Address,
            Product,
            Amount
        FROM

TestTable.xlsx
(ooxml, embedded labels, table is TestTable)
Where WildMatch (Address,'*O*');

Q. How to make the code reusable?
Ans.
Following steps can be taken to make the code reusable.
- Use QVD where ever possible. QVDs can be shared between applications or teams.
- Use **Include** files for any reusable code like database connection string.
- Perform all the calculations in the variables. Store all the variables in a text or excel file. This file can be included in any application.
- Use Binary load to include data model scripts in multiple applications

Q. What technique should be applied to load the following table?
Ans.

Location	2013	2014	2015
Athens	200	300	100
Atlanta	100	200	300
Rome	400	500	300

- The above table is a Crosstable.
- **Crosstable** is a data structure where data in a table is represented in rows and columns.
- Intersection of rows and column is summarized data.
- If Crosstable is loaded using the regular load statement, it will create a separate list for each of the columns. It will utilize huge memory. Aggregation over dimensions will be difficult.
- Crosstable can be transformed into a desirable straight table by using **Crosstable** keyword before the load statement. **CrossTable** (Year, Sales).

- CrossTable is loaded in a similar way as loading the Table files. Select **Enable Transformation Step** after selecting the file.
- Specify Qualifier, Attribute and Data fields.
- **Qualifier** is the leftmost field/s in the table, in this case, Location, which is not to be transformed, **Attribute** field contains the columns, in this case, Years and **Data** field contains the summarized data of the attribute field.

Location	Year	Sales
Athens	2013	200
Athens	2014	300
Athens	2015	300
Atlanta	2013	100
Atlanta	2014	200
Atlanta	2015	300
Rome	2013	400
Rome	2014	500
Rome	2015	300

Q. Explain Section Access
Ans.
- Section Access is implemented to provide data level security to the document.
- Objective of Section Access is to limit the document to only authorized user and also to restrict authorized user to the permitted data.
- It is implemented by using **Hidden Script** in the QVW. Hidden script option can be seen in the script editor, under the file menu.
- All Access control fields can be loaded similar to any other data load in QlikView i.e. through Inline load, text file or database table.
- All data must be loaded in upper case.
- The access control also contains **OMIT** and Reduction fields. Fields mentioned under OMIT will be hidden from the user.

- If Reduction field is mentioned, users will be reduced to only viewing data restricted by the reduce field
- User with Admin access can see all the data

Q. What are Tags?
Ans. Tags can be used to suggest which fields can be used as dimensions or measures in the charts.
Fields can be assigned Dimension and Measure tags by navigating to menu/settings/Document properties - table.
Tags are useful in creating charts with large number of dimensions and measures. By the use of Tags, dimension fields and measures fields will appear together.

Q. What is an Inline table?
Ans.
Inline table is a table created within QlikView. This table does not exist in the data source. Inline table can be created by using Inline load in the script.

Q. You are creating a residential dashboard, but your data source does not contain Property type. How can you create such a table in QlikView
Ans.
Property type table can be created in QlikView by using Inline load script. This table is like any other table in QlikView and can be linked to other tables if common field name exist

```
PropertyType:
Load * Inline [
  PropertyID, PropertyDesc
  ID1, SingleFamily
  ID2, Condos
   ID3, Apartment
     ];
```

Q. What is the difference between of RecNo and RowNo functions?
Ans.
- RecNo() returns the number of the currently read row from the source table. The first record is number 1
- RowNo() returns the integer for the position of the current row in the resulting QlikView internal table.
- RowNo does not count the records which are excluded by the where clause
- RowNo is not reset if source table is concatenated to another table.

Q. See the load statements below. What will be the resulting table?

Table3:
Load * Inline [
    ID, Product
    1, P1
    2, P2
    3, P4
    4, P5
    5, P6
    ];

Table1:
Load * Inline [
    ID, Product
    1, P1
    2, P2
    3, P4
    4, P5
    5, P6
    ];

Table2:
Load
    *,

RecNo()   As RecNo,
RowNo()   As RowNo
Resident Table3
Where ID <> 4;

Drop Table Table3;

Ans.
The resulting table will be
Table2

ID	Product	RecNo	RowNo
1	P1	1	1
2	P2	2	2
3	P4	3	3
5	P6	5	4
1	P1	6	5
2	P2	7	6
3	P4	8	7
6	P6	10	8

Q. Perform Inline load for Table1 below and use the resident load to load RecNo() and RowNo(). What will be the resulting table?

Table1:

ID	Product
1	P1
2	P2
3	P3
4	P4
5	P5

Resident Load statement with RecNo() and RowNo()
Table2:

Load
*,
RecNo()   As RecNo,
RowNo()   As RowNo

Resident Table1

;

Drop Table Table1;

Ans.

The resulting table will be

Table2

ID	Product	RecNo	RowNo
1	P1	1	1
2	P2	2	2
3	P3	3	3
4	P4	4	4
5	P5	5	5

Q. Load the below table and perform resident load as given. What will be the resulting table?

Table1:

ID	Product
1	P1
2	P2
3	P3
4	P4
5	P5

Load statement with RecNo() and RowNo()

Table2:

Load

*,

RecNo()   As RecNo,

RowNo()   As RowNo

Resident Table1

Where ID <> 4

;

Drop Table Table1;

Ans.

The resulting table will be

Table2

ID	Product	RecNo	RowNo
1	P1	1	1
2	P2	2	2
3	P4	3	3
5	P5	5	4

Q. What is Include statement in QlikView?

Ans.

Include statement is used to include external files in QlikView. These files may be database connection files, or any other files used in the development.

Q. How to debug QlikView scripts?

Ans.

- Scripts should be organized in different tabs.
- Related tables should be loaded on the same tab.
- Write comments where ever possible. Comments will help in understanding the scripts.
- If multiple tables are to be loaded, load one table at a time.
- Use **Trace** function to write the statements to the script execution window.
- Invoke Debug option from the script editor.

Chapter 3.
Questions on QlikView designer

Q. How dimensions are displayed on a QlikView dashboard?
Ans.
List box and Multi box can be created on a dashboard to display dimensions.

Q. What chart types are available in QlikView?
Ans.
QlikView provides different kinds of visualization objects. Some of the charts which can be used are

- **Bar chart.** For comparing data elements over dimension/s. Bar charts can also be stacked.
- **Line Chart.** To display the trend of measure over time use Line chart.
- **Combo chart.** It is a combination of bar and line chart and is used to display two measures. One measure can be an amount and another percentage.
- **Straight table.** Used to show the dimensions and expressions.
- **Pivot table.** It is used to display dimension and expressions. Expressions are grouped by dimensions. It is similar to cross table. Pivot table can have subtotals.
- **Scatter chart.** Is used to display relationships between the data elements.
- **Pie Chart.** The pie chart is used to display the slices of the total.
- **Mini charts.** Mini charts or sparklines are used to show the trends. They are displayed for each row of the straight table and created in Straight table/expressions.
- **Gauge chart.** This chart is used to see if the measure falls within or outside a threshold.

Q. What data elements are required to create a chart?
Ans.
Most of the charts require one or more dimensions and one or more expressions.

Q. How to create a simple bar chart
Ans.

- Load TestTable, if it's not already loaded.
- Right click on the QlikView sheet. Select the option to create New Sheet Object and Chart.
- Bar chart is selected by default. Click next and select/add Year as dimension.
- Click next and specify Sum (Amount) as an expression and click finish.

Q. What is the difference between a Table box, Pivot and Straight table?
Ans.

- Table box can contain fields from one or multiple tables. Table box does not contain calculations.
- Straight table consists of a dimension and an expression. Straight tables have interactive sorting.

Pivot table is similar to cross tables. They display dimensions and expressions in rows and columns. Pivot table is grouped by dimension.

Q. How to change the display of a chart by different dimensions
Ans.
A chart can be seen by multiple unrelated dimensions by creating a cyclic group

Q. How to drill down from Year to Quarter and Month
Ans.
A drill down group can be created with the hierarchy as Year, Quarter and Month. Drill down group can be created within the chart or from the Settings/Document properties/Groups.

Q. How to perform Year by Year comparisons in dashboard
Ans.
Year to Year comparisons can be done using Set Analysis.

Q. What is comparative analysis and how it is implemented?
Ans.
Comparative analysis involves comparing data between two time periods or two states.
Comparative analysis can be implemented using Set Analysis and Alternate state.

Q. You have 2 charts and some list boxes. What configuration you will use so that selections made in list box changes data in only one chart and other chart data is not affected by the selections made in the list box.
Ans.
Use **Alternate states**. Keep specific charts and list boxes in a specific state.

Q. What is Set Analysis?
Ans.
- The set Analysis expression is applied in the visualization objects, such as Charts and Text boxes.
- A QlikView document is always in the current state and performs aggregation of the records defined by the current selection.
- Set Analysis is used, any time aggregation is required for the records outside current selection.
- For e.g. the current selection will display Sum (Amount) for the selected year. Use Set Analysis expression, if you want Sum (Amount) for the previous year, next Year or specific Year.
- In the absence of Set Analysis, use of complex if then else statement will be required.
- Set Analysis expression starts and ends with a curly bracket.
- Set Analysis has 3 components – Identifiers, Modifiers and operators.

Q. What are Identifiers in Set Analysis?
Ans.

- The identifier is one of the components in Set Analysis. Other two components are Modifier and Operator.
- Identifiers define a set or defines the scope of the expression. For example $ means current selection. 1 means entire dataset.
- When used in an expression for e.g.,
  Sum ({$} Amount) means Amount for the current selection. $ is optional and is always applied by default as it means current selection.
  Sum ({1} Amount) means total Amount for the entire data in an application. It will not consider the selection made in the list box but will honor the dimensions in the chart where it is used.

Q. What are modifiers?
Ans.
A set can be modified by using Modifiers. It is used like a where clause. In the below example, modifier is used to display Amount where Product = Shirt

Sum ({<Product = {'Shirt'} >} Amount)

Q. Dashboard displays list boxes for a Year, Name and Product. What will be the syntax of Set Analysis expression for displaying Sum (Amount) where Year = 2012, and ignoring the any selection for the Product in the list box?
Ans.

Sum ({<Year = {'2012'}, Product = >} Amount)

Q. What is What-if analysis and how it is implemented?

Ans.

What-if scenario involves accepting user input in the dashboard and changing the calculations based on user input. For e.g., a user wants to know at run time, if he changes the discount price how his overall profitability will change. User can enter different discount prices in the dashboard.

User input is accepted by using **an input box, Slider** and **Input field.**

Q. What is the use of Total Qualifier?

Ans.

In a table/chart, the expression is always calculated by dimension. By using **Total** Qualifier, you can ignore the dimension in the chart. If chart contains multiple dimensions and you want to include specific dimensions, specify those dimensions with Total.

Q. If you have a dimension, say, Dim with values A, B, C and a measure, say Sales with values 100,200,300

How you achieve the following

| Total Qualifier | | | 旦 XL ▁ ☐ |
Dim	Sales by Dim	Total Sales	Dim/Total Sales
	600	600	1.00
A	100	600	0.17
B	200	600	0.33
C	300	600	0.50

Ans.

- The first calculation Sale by Dim is just *Sum (Sales)*
- To perform the second calculation, Total Sales, you need to ignore the dimension Dim. This can be done by using **Total qualifier**. Second expression will be Sum (Total Sales)
- Third expression is Column (1) / Column (2)

Q. How variables are declared in QlikView

Ans.

- In QlikView, variables are declared using **SET** and **LET** statements.
- Variables can be declared in a script or from menu settings/Variable overview.
- SET statement is used to set a value of a variable. This can be used to define today's date or path of a QVD, include files etc.
- The LET statement evaluates the expression on the right side of the = and assigns it to the variables. These variables are used for calculations.
- All defined variables can be seen in Variable Overview.

Q. How will you perform dynamically show/hide of charts?

Ans.

Dynamic show and hide of charts can be implemented by the use of variables and text boxes.

The idea is to show/hide the chart when the user clicks on a button.

1. Create a **chart** which you want to show or hide
2. Create a **variable**, for e.g., Show_Hide in menu settings/Variable overview. Set its value to 1.
3. Create a **Text Object**.
4. In Text Object properties, do the following
   - Under **Actions**, choose **Action Type** as External and **Action** as Set Variable
   - Under **Variable**, give the name of your variable i.e. Show_Hide.
   - Under **value** give the expression as
     If (Show_Hide = 0,1,0)

5. Go to **chart**, created in step 1. Under properties, navigate to the **Layout** tab and under Conditional edit box, provide condition as Show_Hide=1

Q. If the chart contains large amounts of data, how you will force a user from making a selection in the list box, before rendering the chart.

Ans.

Many times, a chart may contain large amounts of data. If this chart is rendered without filter or list box selection, then it may crash the application.

It is good practice in such a scenario to force a user to make at least one selection in the list box.

This can be achieved by using the **Calculation Condition** on the **General** tab of the Chart.

Q. Refer to TestTable which is loaded in the earlier exercise. The requirement is that the user should make a selection in the ID list box before rendering the chart.

Ans.

- Load TestTable if it is not already loaded.
- Create list box for ID.
- Create a straight table, with dimensions as ID, Name, Product and Year.
- In expression, specify Sum (Amount).
- Navigate to the **General** tab of the chart.
- In the **Calculation Condition** specify
  GetSelectedCount (ID) > 0
- Next, click on **Error Messages** on the **General** tab and provide a **custom message** such as "Please select at least one ID to display the chart".

The error message text will show the users that they are expected to select an ID from the list box. Now chart will be displayed only when ID is selected in the list box.

Q. What are mini charts and how to create them?
Ans.
Mini charts are charts which are displayed per row in a straight table. These are created by navigating to the **expressions** tab in straight table and selecting **Representation** as **Mini Chart** under **Display Options**.

Q. Can you create a bar chart without dimension? What will happen if you don't use a dimension in a bar chart?
Ans.
Bar chart shows the intersection of dimension and expression, i.e. if you have a dimension with values A, B and C and an expression say, Sum (Sales) then Sum (Sales) will be displayed for each of the dimensions. You will have 3 bars in the chart.
If a chart is created without the dimension, then it will show one bar with an aggregated value of Sales.
To try this scenario, execute the following Inline load script

Table1:
Load * Inline [
Dim1, Sales
A, 100
B, 200
C, 300
];

Create a 2 bar charts, using Dim1 as dimension and Sum (Sales) as an expression. In one chart use Dim1 as dimension and in another chart don't use any dimension, just use the expression. See the difference

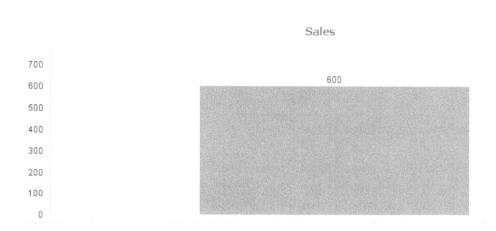

Sales

Chart without dimension

Q. Which chart has only expression and is not affected by dimension?
Ans.
Gauge chart. Dimension in a gauge chart will have no effect on the chart. Dimension is not required.

Q. How you will create an application for mobile devices like iPad?
Ans.
QlikView does not have any specific objects for iPad. For iPad, a dashboard should be developed using the same objects, but for a different screen resolution. The focus should be given to objects that will be more visible on iPad. For e.g. **containers** should be used instead of displaying charts separately.

Q. Explain Aggr function
Ans.
Aggr function comes under advanced aggregation in QlikView. It allows aggregation over dimensions. It is similar to Group By in SQL. Aggr function is also required if nested aggregation functions are used in an expression.

Q. Using TestTable data, write Aggr function expression that will group Sum (Amount) by Product and Year

Ans.

- Create a straight table, with dimensions as ID, Name, Product and Year
- In expression, specify
  Aggr(Sum(Amount),Year, Product)

Q. What is calculated dimension?

Ans.

Charts in QlikView require dimensions. Dimensions provide context to measure or expressions. Sometimes these dimensions exist in the data and sometimes need to be calculated. Such dimensions are called **calculated dimensions**. Calculated dimensions are created in the chart, by using "Add Calculated Dimension" or by simply editing the existing dimension. The calculated dimension can be an expression using conditional statements and functions.

Q. What are synthetic dimensions?

Ans.

Synthetic dimensions are the dimensions which are created by the developer using the synthetic functions. These dimensions are not based on the fields present in the data model.

ValueList and ValueLoop functions are used to create Synthetic dimensions.

Q. How to format a number in a Text Object?

Ans.

Text Object does not have a Number property. In Text Object use NUM() to format a number

Q. What are triggers in QlikView desktop?

Ans. **Triggers** are used to set **Action** on an event. These Actions execute when a specific condition is met.

Trigger types are Document event trigger, Field event trigger and variable event trigger.

The trigger is configured from menu Settings/Document properties and selecting Triggers tab.

Q. My dashboard uses TestTable data. I have a list box for a Product, with values Shirt, Pant and Socks. Create a functionality where clicking on a text object, a selection for "Pant" is made in the Product list box

Ans.

- Right click on the dashboard screen, select New Sheet Object and create a Text object. Label it "Select a Product"
- Go to Text object properties and navigate to **Actions** tab.
- Click on Add and under **Action Type, select Selection** and in the **Action** selection Select in the field
- In the **Field** edit box, type Product and in the **Search string** edit box type Pant
- Click ok

Now the Text object will behave like a button and clicking on it will select "Pant" in the Product list box.

Q. Use TestTable data. In a straight table, If Amount is below or equal to 200 display it in red and if Amount is above 200, display it in green

Ans.

Create a straight table with a required dimension and expression. In the expression for Sum (Amount), collapse the expression by clicking on the + sign on the left. It will open up options for background color, text color and so on. Write following expressions for Text color

If (Sum (Amount) >200, Green (), Red ())

Chapter 4.
Questions on QlikView server admin

Q. What is QlikView Server (QVS) and Publisher?
Ans.
QlikView server hosts all the QlikView documents, users and objects. QlikView server is accessed by QlikView management console.
QlikView publisher is a component of QVS and is used for content management, access, data reduction and distribution. A separate license is required for Publisher.

Q. How QlikView applications are deployed on the server?
Ans.
- QVWs are developed using QlikView desktop and placed in the **Source document** folder. Source document folder is a physical folder on the QlikView Server.
- QVWs will contain data load scripts and/or Visualizations.
- Server folders are accessed through QlikView management console (QMC).
- Appropriate security is applied to the dashboard.
- Data reload and distribution tasks are created.
- Once the distribution tasks are executed, dashboard goes in **User document** folder. Based on the settings one document can be split into multiple documents.
- User access these documents/dashboards from user document folder through **Access Point.**

Q. What are tasks and Trigger on QlikView Management Console?
Ans.
Tasks are created to reload data and distribute dashboards to the users. Triggers are created to schedule a task to run at a certain time. Dependencies between the tasks are also set using triggers.

Q. What different services are available in the QlikView Server environment?
Ans.
- QlikView Management Service (QMS)

QMS manages all the components of the environment. All the communication passes through QMS. Settings of QMS are stored as XML files.

- QlikView Server (QVS)
  It is responsible for handling users, the security of documents, authorization and processes user requests.
- QlikView WebServer (QVWS)
  It is responsible to start user authentication. It also stores Access Point and AJAX client files.
- QlikView distribution services (QDS)
  It performs all the publisher tasks and is also required when the publisher is not present. It reloads data, performs data reduction and distributes documents.
- Directory Service Connector (DSC)
  It is responsible for extracting permission related user information from Active directory, LDAP and ODBC. It also provides email distribution information to QDS.

Q. What different tabs are present in the QlikView Management console?
Ans.
Different tabs present on QlikView Management console are

- **Status**. This tab displays the status of the executed **tasks**. You can monitor the success and failure of the tasks. It also gives the status on different services running on the server.
- **Documents**. This contains subtabs for **Source** and **User Document** folders. Source documents contain developer created dashboards and user document folder contain published dashboard.
- **Users**. This tab is used to configure users and Client Access Licenses
- **System**. This tab contains information regarding the QlikView Server environment and different services.

Q. What is Loop and Reduce in QlikView?
Ans.

Loop and reduce is implemented by QlikView publisher. Using Loop and reduce a single document in the **Source document folder** is split into multiple user documents based on the reduce field. For e.g. if user group is divided into multiple regions, then you will create one dashboard and define loop and reduce based on the reduce field "Region". One QlikView document will be split into multiple documents based on the number of regions. You can even specify the document name prefixed by Regions.

Q. What are CALs? What are the different types of CALs in QlikView?
Ans.

CALs refer to **Client Access License**. To connect to QlikView server, you must have a Client Access License.
There are different CAL types. CAL will depend on the various usage requirements.

- Named User CAL. It is specific to the user or the machine
- Document CAL. It allows users to view only one specific document.
- Session CAL. Allows multiple users to access multiple documents.
- Usage CAL. It gives users the ability to initiate one session i.e. accessing one document per 28-day period.

Q. Does the QlikView server environment always come with a publisher?
Ans.

QlikView implementations can be done in QlikView Server only mode or with a QlikView Server / publisher. Publisher license is purchased separately.
System/License tab displays the details about the Server license.

Q. In the absence of the QlikView publisher license, how many sub-tabs are displayed under the Documents tab in QMC?
Ans.
If Publisher license is not present, only User Documents sub-tab is visible. With a publisher license, both Source document and user document are visible.

Q. How look and feel of Access point can be customized?
Ans.
Access point is a portal where dashboards are displayed. The look and feel of the Access point can be customized by modifying the Access point files. These files are located in the web server installation path.

Q. What is leasing of license?
Ans.
QlikView user using QlikView desktop can lease/borrow a license from the server. This license is available for a period of 30days.Each time QlikView is launched, it tries to reconnect to the server and renew the license lease. If the client does not connect to the server for 30days the license lease expires.
License can be leased from QlikView desktop by "Open in Server"option

Chapter 5.
Commonly Asked
Questions

Q. In an organization, data is updated monthly. Few thousand rows of data get added every month to the existing tables. How you will load this data so that most updated data is reflected in the dashboard?

Ans.

This data load can be done by creating an incremental load script. Using incremental load one can load only the updated rows of data.

Q. Recently we merged into a new company. We want to merge their employee data into our employee table. How can we achieve this?

Ans.

Both the tables should have the same structure. You can load both the tables in QlikView and concatenate them. This will append new employee records into the existing employee table

Q. We have different departments developing dashboards. How to make sure that dashboards will show a single version of the truth and enterprise solution is delivered

Ans.

Following practices will ensure the enterprise level of implementation

- The data model should be created once and should be included in the presentation layer by the use of Binary Load.
- Use QVDs for data storage and extraction in QlikView.
- Create Master QVDs for the data which can be reused by different teams. Examples for such QVDs can be Master calendar or Organization Info.
- Data source connection info should be kept in a text file and should be included in the dashboard using the Include statement.

- All standardized calculations should be maintained outside the dashboards by using variables. All commonly used calculations/variables should be kept in a text file or excel file. This calculation variable file should be included in the dashboard using the Include command.
- Look and feel of the dashboard should be the same. Create a QlikView template file which should be used by all the developers to create dashboards.
- Create a dashboard review board that will review all the dashboards before moving to production.

Q. An organization has around 100 users. What kind of CALs /license configuration should be implemented?
Ans.
CALs should always be assigned based on the requirement of the users. We should know how users will be utilizing QlikView and how frequently. Users accessing the QlikView dashboards on a daily basis should get Named CALs. The more infrequent users can share the sessions CALs.

Q. How to setup QlikView development environment?
Ans.
For ease and organized QlikView development
- Folder structure should be setup. This folder structure should have folders for
  - Apps – This folder contains Qvw files.
  - Data – This folder should contain subfolders for all the data, such as excel files, text file, QVDs etc.
  - Include – This folder should contain files to be included i.e. database connections, variables, any other.
  - Template – This should contain QlikView template files. There can be more than one template file based on the screen resolution.
- QlikView Desktop Settings should be configured to Generate log files, save before reload and other require settings.

Q. What common tasks can be performed using QlikView management console?

Ans.

Some of the tasks performed using QMC are

- Connect to QlikView Server.
- Create data reload and distribution tasks.
- Schedule triggers to run the data load and distribution tasks at a specified time.
- Monitor status to view the success and failures of the different tasks.
- Monitored various services in the QlikView Server environment.
- Implement security and data reduction.

Q. How to implement QlikView multi-developer environment?

Ans.

Multi-developer environment is required when the number of dashboards are to be developed by different developers.

In such an implementation, the team can be divided into data modelers and dashboard designers. Alternatively, one complete dashboard can be assigned to a single developer. But when the dashboard is huge then multiple developers can work on the same dashboard.

There can be many ways to implement such scenarios

- Data modeler/s create data models.
- Binary load is used by the dashboard developers to incorporate this data model scripts in the dashboard.
- If the dashboard is big, developers can be assigned to design specific sheets or charts.
- Team lead or a person assigned can merge all the separate charts into one main dashboard by copying and pasting.
- To manage such an environment, shared folders can be created.

Q. How to test a QlikView application?
Ans.
QlikView application should be tested at multiple levels. If multi-tier data architecture is implemented, then extract layer, transform layer and presentation layer should be tested. The basic principle is to always compare against the source data

- In Extract layer, after each table is loaded. Check it against the original data source. Check the count of rows in QlikView table and the source table.
- In Transform layer, check against the source table. If source is a database then write SQL queries to compare the results. Check aggregations after the transformation is done in QlikView tables.
- In the final data model, check for Information density and subset ratio. **Information density** gives the number of Not-Null records as compared to the total number of records in the table. **Subset ratio** is the number of distinct values of a field in a table as compared to the total number of distinct values of this field in other tables.
- Create a Table box of the table loaded and export it to excel to perform data validations.
- In the presentation layer, compare visualization created with the user requirements. To test calculations and aggregations, create Text Object to display calculations and aggregations.
- Check the aggregations in the charts by writing SQL in the database. For excel data sources, use excel filters and formulas.

Q. What should be the size of a QVD or QVW?
Ans.
The size of the QVD and QVW depends on the specific requirement. There is no fixed size. The size of the dashboard depends on the data, objects and functionality of the dashboard.

Q. How you will open a QVW bigger than 4GB in size?

Ans.

If the dashboard size is larger than the RAM size of your computer, then you can open it on the server which will have more RAM. Alternatively, if development is in progress and you don't need the complete data, then perform limited load by using the debug option of the script editor.

Q. How much time it takes to create a dashboard?

Ans.

There is no fix or set time to create a dashboard. Dashboard creation time always depends on the complexity of the requirement. Simple dashboards can be created in few minutes.

Q. What best practices should be followed in QlikView data modeling?

Ans.

Use the following to create an effective data model

- Use QVD for good performance.
- Create 3 tier data architecture viz. Extract layer, transformation layer and presentation layer.
- Rename data source columns to give user friendly names.
- Remove synthetic keys and loops.
- Perform all the complex calculations in the script.
- Create Master calendar to handle dates.
- Use optimized load in the presentation layer for better performance.

Q. In a multiple-tier QVD architecture, you have extract layer and transform layer. Which layer will have a smaller QVD size?

Ans.

Transform layer will have a smaller QVD size. In the transform layer, some transformation or filters must have been applied. Extract layer generally contains raw data.

Q. How to performance tune QlikView data model and dashboard?

Ans.

Some of the ways to improve performance is to

- Use QVDs where ever possible.
- Reduce number of tables by using Mapping load, concatenate, join, qualify, link table as appropriate.
- Reduce synthetic keys and loops.
- Avoid using count distinct.
- Avoid using calculated dimensions.
- If date column contains the time information and time information is not required, remove the time information by using floor() function.
- Perform incremental load to load only new and updated data in the tables.

Q. Does Set Analysis occurs always in QlikView expression?

Ans.

Yes. Set Analysis always occurs in QlikView expressions. For e.g., When Sum (Amount) is used in an expression, it is actually executing Sum ({$} Sales) $ is by default for current selection and is optional.

Q. There are 10 users and they want to see data only pertaining to them. How you will achieve this. You will create 10 dashboards or one dashboard

Ans.

This will be done by creating one dashboard, but assigning security to users based on Section Access.

Q. What best practices should be followed while creating a dashboard?

Ans.

While creating a dashboard, care should be given so that the dashboard is clean and easy to understand. Following practices can be followed

- Design dashboard for a specific Screen resolution. Discuss with your user community and decide on a screen resolution that will cater to all the users
- Design a Screen layout which makes the navigation on the screen natural and easy. The basic structure is list boxes on the left. Time related list boxes on the top center. Charts and tables in the middle of the screen.
- Avoid using complex calculations in the dashboard. Move such calculations to the script.
- Use muted colors. So that focus is in the dashboard not on the color.
- Create a template and include all the layout related attributes on this template. Use this template to develop the dashboards.

Q. What are the responsibilities of a QlikView professional?
Ans.
QlikView consultant or developer's responsibilities may differ based on specific organization, but at high-level it consists of
- Understanding the requirements.
- Extracting data and creating a data model by applying required transformations.
- Creating dashboards by using different objects such as charts, text boxes etc. for data analysis.
- Deploying the dashboards on the server.

Q. How you will gain an understanding of an already developed QlikView application?
Ans.
To understand an existing application,
- See what data elements, objects, sheets are displayed on the dashboard.
- Use System fields to understand the data loaded in the dashboard. System fields are prefixed by $ and can be used to create list box.

- Variable overview and Expression overview will give details on the variables and expression used in the application.
- Settings/Document settings will give details on the sheets used. It will also show details on the hidden sheets.
- Document settings will also provide details on different sheet objects, groups, triggers etc. used in the development.
- A look at the Table Viewer will show the tables loaded and relationship between them.
- To understand scripts, invoke the script editor and review each tab. Execute only one tab and comment other tabs. Load one table at a time.

About The Author

AUTHOR NAME is Chandraish Sinha
Find out more at amazon.com/author/ChandraishSinha
Or visit www.LearnAllBi.com

Can I Ask A Favor?
If you enjoyed this book, found it useful or otherwise, then I'd really appreciate it if you would post a short review on Amazon. I do read all the reviews personally so that I can continually write what people are wanting.
Thanks for your support!

www.ingramcontent.com/pod-product-compliance
Lightning Source LLC
Chambersburg PA
CBHW061033050326
40689CB00012B/2805